Playing w
Pre
Shake

Macbeth

(The melodramatic version!)

For 6-17+ actors, or kids of all ages who want to have fun!
Creatively modified by Brendan P. Kelso
Cover illustrated by Shana Lopez
Edited by Hannah Sidaris-Green

3 Melodramatic Modifications of Shakespeare's Play
for 3 different group sizes:

6-9

9-12

12-17+

Table Of Contents

To Keagan:
Who fights against great odds to make my life wonderful.

-Dad

Playing with Plays™ - Shakespeare's Macbeth - for Kids

Copyright © 2004-2009 by Brendan P. Kelso, Playing with Publishing

www.PlayingWithPlays.com

Printed in the United States of America

Published by: Playing with Publishing

ISBN: 1-4392-1353-4
ISBN: 9781439213537

Foreword

When I was in high school there was something about Shakespeare that appealed to me. Not that I understood it mind you, but there were clear scenes and images that always stood out in my mind. Romeo & Juliet, "Romeo, Romeo; wherefore art thou Romeo?"; Julius Caesar, "Et tu Brute"; Macbeth, "Double, Double, toil and trouble"; Hamlet, "to be or not to be"; A Midsummer Night's Dream, all I remember about this was a wickedly cool fairy and something about a guy turning into a donkey that I thought was pretty funny. It was not until I started analyzing Shakespeare's plays as an actor that I realized one very important thing, I still didn't understand them. Seriously though, it's tough enough for adults, let alone kids. Then it hit me, why don't I make a version that kids could perform, but make it easy for them to understand with a splash of Shakespeare lingo mixed in? And viola! A melodramatic masterpiece was created!

The entire purpose of this book is to instill the love of acting and Shakespeare into kids. I initially wrote my first Shakespeare play (Hamlet) to teach a few kids how to have fun with Shakespeare. It has evolved into a revolving door of new and returning kids constantly wanting more and more Shakespeare, from kids asking for the entire Shakespeare anthology for Christmas to writing a report in their 2nd grade class on heroes and choosing Shakespeare. Shakespeare is difficult enough when you are an adult, let alone a teenager (I didn't have a clue what Julius Caeser was about, except for "Et tu Brute!"). But for kids, most people (those calling themselves "adults" mind you) told me to forget it, "you can't teach kids Shakespeare". Well, I will have you know, that not only do these kids love Shakespeare now, they want more of it! And when you have children who have a passion for something, they will start to teach themselves, with or without school.

THE PLAYS: There are 3 plays within this book, for three different group sizes. The reason: to allow educators or parents to get the story across to their children regardless of the size of their group. Experienced actor variation: If you read any Shakespeare play as an actor you will notice one very common occurrence – NO STAGE DIRECTIONS. Okay, it happens occasionally, but it's very rare. Any actor with creative skills will tell you that this is a wonderful thing: it leaves full interpretation to the actor. Therefore, for the children who wish to explore their creative side, I suggest taking the play and whiting out ALL of the stage directions, allowing for the more experienced actors to be as creative as they want to be.

These plays are intended for pure fun. Please DO NOT have the kids learn these lines verbatim, that would be a complete waste of creativity. But do have them basically know their lines and improvise wherever they want as long as it pertains to telling the story, because that is the goal of an actor: to tell the story. In A Midsummer Night's Dream, I once had a student playing Quince question me about one of her lines, "but in the actual story, didn't the Mechanicals state that 'they would hang us'?" I thought for a second and realized that she had read the story with her mom, and she was right. So I let her add the line she wanted and it added that much more fun, it made the play theirs. I have had kids throw water on the audience, run around the audience, sit in the audience, lose their pumpkin pants (size 30 around a size 15 doesn't work very well, but makes for some great humor!) and most importantly, die all over the stage. The kids love it.

I have a basic formula that I use for these plays:
Day 1: I perform my own solo 5-minute Shakespeare play (I am totally winded by the end of it, because I have been all over the set and have died a few times if I can fit it in); we all read through the play together (randomly handing out parts); then auditions – and all auditions MUST include the actors best dieing scenes (they love this the most and will line up again and again to die on stage); the other is for the screams, they love this too, but don't forget to bring earplugs, they will be incredibly loud for both girls and boys since not all have come of age yet.
Day 2: Parts are given out; we read through the play again with our new parts; start blocking
Day 3: finish blocking; rehearse
Day 4: rehearse-no scripts
Day 5: rehearse; try on costumes, and dress rehearsal
Day 6: 2 Dress rehearsals and then performance.
This can easily be stretched to an 8 day course with the 2 extra days used for more rehearsal; set design; invitation creation; makeup practice; etc. As any director will tell you, actors can always use more rehearsal.

THE BARD'S WORK: As you read through the plays, there are several lines that are highlighted. These are actual lines from Shakespeare's text. I am a little more particular about the kids saying these lines verbatim. We need to do these correctly because we don't want to upset Willie. I find that there are many benefits to having these lines in there:

1. Kids are so cute when they are spouting Shakespeare.
2. Parents love to know that their kids are learning actual Shakespeare verbiage.
3. Most lines are very famous lines that they will come across later in life (to be or not to be; Romeo, Romeo, wherefore art thou; double, double toil and trouble; etc.)
4. The kids tend to feel they are more important when they are saying Shakespeare's lines.
5. The lines are easy to understand, giving the kids confidence that they will understand more Shakespeare lines later in life.

One last note: if you loved our plays, want to tell the world how much your kids loved performing Shakespeare, or are just a fan of Shakespeare, then hop on our website and have fun:

PlayingWithPlays.com

With these notes I bid you adieu, have fun, and good luck!

The 10-Minute or so Macbeth
By William Shakespeare
Creatively modified by Brendan P. Kelso
6-9 Actors

CAST OF CHARACTERS

MACBETH – Thane of Glamis – the good guy, then the bad guy

LADY MACBETH – really evil wife of Macbeth

BANQUO – Macbeth's friend, then ex-friend

WITCHES* (#1, 2, & 3) – Scary witches with cool lines

DUNCAN** – King of Scotland

MACDUFF – Thane of Fife

SIWARD** – an Earl

*1-3 witches can be played by 1-3 actors

** Duncan and Siward can be played by the same actor

ACT 1 SCENE 1

(WITCHES enter)

WITCHES: Fair is foul, and foul is fair;
Hover through the fog and filthy air.

WITCH #1: When shall we three meet again? In thunder, lightening, or in rain?

WITCH #2: When the hurlyburly's done, When the battle's lost and won.

WITCH #3: Wow, talk about confusion, what did we just say?

WITCH #1: Let's meet again after the war to talk with Macbeth.

WITCHES #3 & #2: Oh....Okay.

(WITCHES exit)

ACT 1 SCENE 2

(DUNCAN enters)

DUNCAN: Hmmmm, I wonder what is going on with the war?

(a scroll, note, paper, or some type of message is thrown/ delivered on stage to DUNCAN)

DUNCAN: Wow, this is better than email! *(reading message)* There was lots of blood and bodies and the Thane of Cawdor is a traitor. But we were saved because for brave Macbeth, well he deserves that name, killed them all and chased the Norwegians out of Scotland!

DUNCAN: *(thinking to himself)* Great, I need to go tell Macbeth that he is now the Thane of Cawdor.

(DUNCAN exits)

ACT 1 SCENE 3

(WITCHES enter and gather around the cauldron. WITCHES do various creepy and gross things)

(MACBETH and BANQUO enter a moment later)

BANQUO: You're my good buddy, Macbeth.

MACBETH: Mine too, Banquo.

BANQUO: Friends forever!

MACBETH: Yeah! *(they high five or do some other special handshake)*

BANQUO: Look at these crazy looking old hags. So withered and so wild in their attire.

MACBETH: Yeah, they're pretty creepy *(sniffs one)* and smelly too!

WITCHES: Hey Macbeth!

MACBETH: Yeah?

WITCH #1: All hail, Macbeth! hail to thee, Thane of Glamis!

WITCH #2: All hail, Macbeth! hail to thee, Thane of Cawdor!

WITCH #3: All hail, Macbeth! that shalt be King hereafter! Of Scotland that is!

BANQUO: That was cool! I want you to tell me my future too!

WITCH #2: Fine, ummm....all your sons will be kings!

BANQUO: Now that's a reading!

MACBETH: But I am only the Thane of Glamis?

WITCHES: Bye-Bye! *(WITCHES exit)*

BANQUO: Whoa! Where did they go? *(looking around, suddenly a scroll, note, paper, or some type of message is thrown/delivered on stage to MACBETH)* Oh look, there is a message for you Macbeth. *(reads from a very long sheet)* "You da man".

MACBETH: What does that mean?

BANQUO: *(still reading)* "It means, since you saved our country, that you are now the Thane of Cawdor and you get all of his goods."

MACBETH: *(aside to audience)* Really....hmmm, those old ladies were right. I wonder what it would be like to be King, I wonder what I would have to do to be King.... oh this could be fun! Come what may.

BANQUO: Mac, what are you thinking over there?

MACBETH: Oh, nothing. *(said with a big fake smile)*

(ALL exit)

ACT 1 SCENE 4

(LADY MACBETH enters)

LADY MACBETH: *(reading letter)* "Dear honey, met some really weird old ladies, they said I would be King, bye." Hmmmmmm....... *(thinking to herself evilly as she walks off stage)* must be mean, must be nasty, cruel, callous, evil, vicious, wicked, malicious, ...oh yeah, and did I mention mean!

(LADY MACBETH exits)

ACT 1 SCENE 5

(Enter DUNCAN, MACBETH, and BANQUO)

DUNCAN: Well hello Thane of Cawdor.

MACBETH: Hello!

DUNCAN: Just want to let you all know, that I am pronouncing my son Malcolm to be the next King when I step down.

MACBETH: *(aside)* No!

DUNCAN: What?

MACBETH: Nothing. *(aside to audience)* Now I have to go through the king and his son. Man, this is going to get messy. Remember, look like the innocent flower, but be the serpent under't.

BANQUO: Mac, what are you thinking over there?

MACBETH: Oh, nothing. *(said with a big fake smile)*

(ALL exit)

ACT 1 SCENE 6

(MACBETH enters; LADY MACBETH is center)

MACBETH: Hi Honey, I'm home!

LADY MACBETH: Okay, I have a plan for you to be King! *(as she snickers evilly)*

MACBETH: Okay.

LADY MACBETH: King's coming over tonight for dinner, I will be serving him a large helping of "your goose is cooked", if you know what I mean.

MACBETH: *(confused)* Ahhh. No, I don't know what you mean.

LADY MACBETH: I am going to serve him his "last meal". If you know what I mean.

MACBETH: Right! *(confused)* Wrong, I don't know what you mean.

LADY MACBETH: *(frustrated)* I am going to serve him food and you are going to kill him. Do you NOW know what I mean?

MACBETH: Right!

(LADY MACBETH and MACBETH evilly laugh together evilly and make evil faces towards the audience. There is a loud knocking.)

LADY MACBETH: That's the king, put on a happy face and let's go! *(both exit)*

ACT 1 SCENE 7

(MACBETH, LADY MACBETH, DUNCAN, and BANQUO are all sitting around eating dinner)

DUNCAN: Great meal Lady Macbeth, you have to send me that recipe.

BANQUO: That really was a great meal.

LADY MACBETH: Well I am glad you enjoyed it. Oh my, look at the time, everyone go to sleep! *(LADY MACBETH shoos everyone out of the room)*

ALL: Okay.

ACT 1 SCENE 8

MACBETH: *(to himself alone on stage)* To be or not to be...... whoops, wrong play. To kill or not to kill.....there we go....if I kill him lots of people will hate me, BUT, if I kill him I will be King. Hmmmm - to kill or not to kill....... *(LADY MACBETH enters)*

LADY MACBETH: So, did you do it?

MACBETH: *(taking a stand)* I have decided that I am not going to do it.

LADY MACBETH: WHAT!? Are you a man? Get on with it!

MACBETH: *(whining)* But do I have to?

LADY MACBETH: Listen here, pull yourself together and go do the deed. I will get the bodyguards drunk and then we will blame them.

MACBETH: Yes, dear. *(as LADY MACBETH puts his dagger in his hands and shoves him off stage)*

ACT 2 SCENE 1

(DUNCAN runs on stage and dies with a dagger stuck in him, MACBETH drags his body off and then returns with the bloody dagger. LADY MACBETH enters)

LADY MACBETH: Did you do it?

MACBETH: *(clueless)* Do what?

LADY MACBETH: KILL HIM!

MACBETH: Oh yeah, all done. I have done the deed.

LADY MACBETH: *(pointing at the dagger)* What is that?

MACBETH: What?

LADY MACBETH: Why do you still have the bloody dagger with you?

MACBETH: Ummmmm, I don't know.

LADY MACBETH: Well, go put it back!

MACBETH: NO! I'm scared of the dark, and there is a dead body in there.

LADY MACBETH: Man you are a wimp, give it to me. *(LADY MACBETH takes the dagger, exits, and returns)*

LADY MACBETH: All done.

(there is a loud knock at the door)

LADY MACBETH: It's 2am! This really is not a good time for more visitors. *(goes to the door)* Who is it? *(opens door)*

MACDUFF: It is Macduff, I am here to see the king.

MACBETH: He is sleeping in there.

(MACDUFF exits)

MACDUFF: *(off stage scream)* AGHHHHHHHHHHHH – He's dead!!! he's dead!!! *(MACDUFF enters)*

MACBETH: Who?

MACDUFF: Who do you think? *(they both scream)*

BANQUO: *(BANQUO enters)* What happened?

MACDUFF: The king has been murdered.

BANQUO: Malcolm, the king's son, heard and left for England.

MACDUFF: Well since there is no one left to be King, why don't you do it Mac?

LADY MACBETH & MACBETH: Okay. *(LADY MACBETH, MACBETH and MACDUFF exit)*

BANQUO: *(To himself)* I fear, Thou play'dst most foully for't *(MACBETH returns)*

MACBETH: Bank, what are you thinking over there?

BANQUO: Oh nothing. *(said with a big fake smile)* Gotta go! See ya! *(BANQUO exits)*

MACBETH: I don't trust Banquo, he knows too much. I need to have my murderer take care of him. *(MACBETH exits offstage)* Hey, Murderer!

ACT 3 SCENE 1

(BANQUO is standing on stage tying his shoe or something like that. A scroll, note, paper, or some type of message is thrown/ delivered on stage to BANQUO)

BANQUO: *(reading message)* You have just been killed by a murderer.

BANQUO: *(to himself and the audience)* You have got to be kidding me. Is this really how I am going to get killed? Really? *(from backstage you hear everyone say, "YES!")* This is embarrassing. *(BANQUO suddenly dies)*

ACT 3 SCENE 2

(MACBETH and LADY MACBETH enter)

MACBETH: Honey, I am really going wacky over all of this killing, greed, and guilt. What am I supposed to do?

LADY MACBETH: Be a man!

MACBETH: Right, what's done is done, there is no turning back now, and I will kill anyone that comes in my way! I must see those crazy witches!

(MACBETH and LADY MACBETH exit)

ACT 4 SCENE 1

(WITCHES enter with Cauldron)

WITCHES: Double, Double toil and trouble,
Fire burn, and cauldron bubble.

WITCH #1: Eye of newt, and toe of frog,
Wool of bat, and tongue of dog.

WITCH #2: Scale of dragon, tooth of wolf,
Witches' mummy, maw and gulf.

WITCH #3: Adder's fork, and blind-worm's sting,
Lizard's leg, and howlet's wing.
By the pricking of my thumbs,
Something wicked this way comes.

(enter MACBETH)

MACBETH: How now, you secret, black, and midnight hags! Tell me what I need to know!

WITCH #1: Macbeth, Macbeth, Macbeth, beware Macduff.

WITCH #2: None of woman born shall harm Macbeth.

WITCH #3: Macbeth will never die until the Great Birnam Wood comes to High Dunsinane Hill

MACBETH: So let me get this straight: a forest that is miles away from a hill has to actually move together, nobody born by a woman can harm me, and I only have to beware of Macduff?

WITCHES: Yep. That's what we said, don't you listen?

MACBETH: *(to himself)* Cool. First I have to kill Macduff and his family!

(ALL exit)

ACT 4 SCENE 2

(MACDUFF enters and addresses audience)

MACDUFF: I am not treacherous, but Macbeth is. I hear Macbeth is being a bully and a tyrant. So I got the King of England to let me borrow his army so I can go over and kick Macbeth's butt!

(a scroll, note, paper, or some type of message is thrown/ delivered on stage to MACDUFF)

MACDUFF: *(reading message)* Macduff, bad news. Your family has been murdered by Macbeth.

MACDUFF: Noooooo! AGGGHHHHHHHHHHHHHHHH!!!!!!!!!!!

(MACDUFF runs of stage screaming and waving his sword)

ACT 5 SCENE 1

(enter LADY MACBETH sleep walking)

LADY MACBETH: *(in sleep walking voice)* Can't wash blood off hands. Out, damned spot! Out I say! Feel guilty about King Duncan, Banquo, Lady Macduff. Husband going nuts. *(repeats constantly untill she exits)*

ACT 5 SCENE 2

(enter MACBETH talking to himself)

MACBETH: I have to kill everyone, no one will stop me from being King. *(looks offstage as if he were looking out a window)* Well now, that is weird. It appears that Birnam Woods is moving closer to our castle here on Dunsinane Hill.

(A loud scream from LADY MACBETH is heard off stage)

MACBETH: What was that? *(looks offstage)* Ahhh man, Lady Macbeth just died. Bummer. Out, out, brief candle! Life's but a walking shadow, a poor player that struts and frets his hour upon the stage and then is heard no more. Eh, she was bugging me anyway. Well, the witches have been right every time. But I think they are wrong this time. I will die fighting!

(enter Siward)

MACBETH: What do you want Young Siward?

SIWARD: I want to kill you Macbeth!

MACBETH: Funny you say that, I can't be killed by a man born from a woman.

SIWARD: Uh oh.

(MACBETH kills Siward)

MACBETH: This is going to be easy.

(enter MACDUFF)

MACBETH: Well, well, well.

MACDUFF: That's a deep subject

MACBETH: I will have you know that I bear a charmed life. I cannot be killed by a man born from a woman.

MACDUFF: Really, that's nice.

MACBETH: *(taken aback)* Why do you say that?

MACDUFF: Because I was plucked from my mom's womb. Achmmm.... what the witches REALLY meant was "no man NATURALLY born from a woman". Stinks to be you.

MACBETH: Uh oh.

(MACDUFF kills MACBETH)

MACDUFF: *(to the audience)* Wow, this is great! We will now all live free of tyranny! We get to have King Duncan's son, Malcom, as the new king! All hail King Malcolm! *(MACDUFF cheers, exits)*

THE END

The 10-Minute or so Macbeth
By William Shakespeare
Creatively modified by Brendan P. Kelso
9-12 Actors

CAST OF CHARACTERS

MACBETH – Thane of Glamis – the good guy, then the bad guy

LADY MACBETH – really evil wife of Macbeth

BANQUO – Macbeth's friend, then ex-friend

WITCHES* (#1, 2, & 3) – Scary witches with cool lines

ROSS – Thane of Ross

DUNCAN** – King of Scotland

MALCOLM – son of King Duncan

MACDUFF – Thane of Fife

MURDERER – a murderer and a really bad guy

SIWARD** – an Earl

*1-3 witches can be played by 1-3 actors

** Duncan and Siward can be played by the same actor

ACT 1 SCENE 1

(WITCHES enter)

WITCHES: Fair is foul, and foul is fair;
Hover through the fog and filthy air.

WITCH #1: When shall we three meet again? In thunder, lightening, or in rain?

WITCH #2: When the hurlyburly's done, When the battle's lost and won.

WITCH #3: Wow, talk about confusion, what did we just say?

WITCH #1: Let's meet again after the war to talk with Macbeth.

WITCHES #3 & #2: Oh....Okay.

(WITCHES exit)

ACT 1 SCENE 2

(DUNCAN and MALCOLM enter)

DUNCAN: Malcolm my son, I wonder what is going on with the war?

MALCOLM: I hear that there was lots of blood and bodies and the Thane of Cawdor is a traitor. But we were saved for brave Macbeth, well he deserves that name, killed them all and chased the Norwegians out of Scotland! Dad, here comes the worthy Thane of Ross.

(ROSS enters)

DUNCAN: Great, Ross, go tell Macbeth that he is now the Thane of Cawdor.

ROSS: Will do.

(ALL exit)

(WITCHES enter and gather around the cauldron. WITCHES do various creepy and gross things)

(MACBETH and BANQUO enter a moment later)

BANQUO: You're my good buddy, Macbeth.

MACBETH: Mine too, Banquo.

BANQUO: Friends forever!

MACBETH: Yeah! *(they high five or do some other special handshake)*

BANQUO: Look at these crazy looking old hags. So withered and so wild in their attire.

MACBETH: Yeah, they're pretty creepy *(sniffs one)* and smelly too!

WITCHES: Hey Macbeth!

MACBETH: Yeah?

WITCH #1: All hail, Macbeth! hail to thee, Thane of Glamis!

WITCH #2: All hail, Macbeth! hail to thee, Thane of Cawdor!

WITCH #3: All hail, Macbeth! that shalt be King hereafter! Of Scotland that is!

BANQUO: That was cool! I want you to tell me my future too!

WITCH #2: Fine, ummm....all your sons will be kings!

BANQUO: Now that's a reading!

MACBETH: But I am only the Thane of Glamis?

WITCHES: Bye-Bye! *(WITCHES exit)*

BANQUO: Whoa! Where did they go? *(looking around)* Look, here comes the worthy Thane of Ross.

(ROSS enters)

MACBETH: Hey Ross.

ROSS: Hello, I have a message for you from the king.... *(reads from a very long sheet)* "You da man".

MACBETH: What does that mean?

ROSS: It means, since you saved our country, that you are now the Thane of Cawdor and you get all of his goods.

MACBETH: *(aside to audience)* Really....hmmm, those old ladies were right. I wonder what it would be like to be King, I wonder what I would have to do to be King.... oh this could be fun! Come what may.

BANQUO: Mac, what are you thinking over there?

MACBETH: Oh, nothing. *(said with a big fake smile)*

(ALL exit)

ACT 1 SCENE 4

(LADY MACBETH enters)

LADY MACBETH: *(reading letter)* "Dear honey, met some really weird old ladies, they said I would be King, bye." Hmmm-mmm....... *(thinking to herself evilly as she walks off stage)* must be mean, must be nasty, cruel, callous, evil, vicious, wicked, malicious, ...oh yeah, and did I mention mean!

(LADY MACBETH exits)

ACT 1 SCENE 5

(Enter DUNCAN, MALCOLM, MACBETH, and BANQUO)

DUNCAN: Well hello, Thane of Cawdor.

MACBETH: Hello!

DUNCAN: Just want to let you all know, that I am pronouncing my son Malcolm to be the next King when I step down.

MALCOLM: Yes!

MACBETH: *(aside)* No!

DUNCAN: What?

MACBETH: Nothing. *(aside to audience)* Now I have to go through the king and his son. Man, this is going to get messy. Remember, look like the innocent flower, but be the serpent under't.

BANQUO: Mac, what are you thinking over there?

MACBETH: Oh, nothing. *(said with a big fake smile)*

(ALL exit)

ACT 1 SCENE 6

(MACBETH enters; LADY MACBETH is center)

MACBETH: Hi Honey, I'm home!

LADY MACBETH: Okay, I have a plan for you to be king! *(as she snickers evilly)*

MACBETH: Okay.

LADY MACBETH: King's coming over tonight for dinner, I will be serving him a large helping of "your goose is cooked", if you know what I mean.

MACBETH: *(confused)* Ahhh. No, I don't know what you mean.

LADY MACBETH: I am going to serve him his "last meal". If you know what I mean.

MACBETH: Right! *(confused)* Wrong, I don't know what you mean.

LADY MACBETH: *(frustrated)* I am going to serve him food and you are going to kill him. Do you NOW know what I mean?

MACBETH: Right!

(LADY MACBETH and MACBETH laugh together evilly and make evil faces towards the audience. There is a loud knocking.)

LADY MACBETH: That's the king, put on a happy face and let's go!

(both exit)

ACT 1 SCENE 7

(MACBETH, LADY MACBETH, DUNCAN, MALCOLM, and BANQUO are all sitting around eating dinner)

DUNCAN: Great meal Lady Macbeth, you have to send me that recipe.

BANQUO: That really was a great meal.

MALCOLM: It sure was!

LADY MACBETH: Well, I am glad you enjoyed it. Oh my, look at the time, everyone go to sleep! *(LADY MACBETH shoos everyone out of the room)*

ALL: Okay.

ACT 1 SCENE 8

MACBETH: *(to himself alone on stage)* To be or not to be...... whoops, wrong play. To kill or not to kill.....there we go....if I kill him lots of people will hate me, BUT, if I kill him I will be King. Hmmmm – to kill or not to kill....... *(LADY MACBETH enters)*

LADY MACBETH: So, did you do it?

MACBETH: *(taking a stand)* I have decided that I am not going to do it.

LADY MACBETH: WHAT!? Are you a man? Get on with it!

MACBETH: *(whining)* But do I have to?

LADY MACBETH: Listen here, pull yourself together and go do the deed. I will get the bodyguards drunk and then we will blame them.

MACBETH: Yes dear. *(as LADY MACBETH puts his dagger in his hands and shoves him off stage)*

ACT 2 SCENE 1

(DUNCAN runs on stage and dies with a dagger stuck in him, MACBETH drags his body off and then returns with the bloody dagger. LADY MACBETH enters)

LADY MACBETH: Did you do it?

MACBETH: *(clueless)* Do what?

LADY MACBETH: KILL HIM!

MACBETH: Oh yeah, all done. I have done the deed.

LADY MACBETH: *(pointing at the dagger)* What is that?

MACBETH: What?

LADY MACBETH: Why do you still have the bloody dagger with you?

PlayingWithPlays.com

MACBETH: Ummmmm, I don't know.

LADY MACBETH: Well, go put it back!

MACBETH: NO! I'm scared of the dark, and there is a dead body in there.

LADY MACBETH: Man you are a wimp, give it to me. *(LADY MACBETH takes the dagger, exits, and returns)*

LADY MACBETH: All done.

(there is a loud knock at the door)

LADY MACBETH: It's 2am! This really is not a good time for more visitors. *(goes to the door)* Who is it? *(opens door)*

MACDUFF: It is Macduff, I am here to see the king.

MACBETH: He is sleeping in there.

(MACDUFF exits)

MACDUFF: *(off stage scream)* AGHHHHHHHHHHHH – He's dead, he's dead!!! *(MACDUFF enters)*

MACBETH: Who?

MACDUFF: Who do you think? *(they both scream)*

BANQUO: *(BANQUO and MALCOLM enter)* What happened?

MACDUFF: The king has been murdered.

MALCOLM: Aghhhhhhhh!!!!!!!! I must be next. I'm getting out of here. I'm off to England. *(MALCOLM exits)*

MACDUFF: Well since there is no one left to be King, why don't you do it Mac?

LADY MACBETH & MACBETH: Okay. *(LADY MACBETH, MACBETH and MACDUFF exit)*

BANQUO: *(To himself)* I fear, Thou play'dst most foully for't *(MACBETH returns)*

MACBETH: Bank, what are you thinking over there?

BANQUO: Oh, nothing. *(said with a big fake smile)* Gotta go! See ya! *(BANQUO exits)*

MACBETH: I don't trust Banquo, he knows too much. *(towards offstage)* Hey Murderer!

MURDERER: *(MURDERER enters)* Yes sir.

MACBETH: Banquo *(makes slash across throat sign)*

MURDERER: Gotcha *(MURDERER and MACBETH exit)*

ACT 3 SCENE 1

(BANQUO is standing on stage tying his shoe or something like that. MURDERER enters)

MURDERER: Hey, you Banquo?

BANQUO: Yeah, who are you?

MURDERER: Murderer.

BANQUO: Uh oh. *(BANQUO is killed)*

ACT 3 SCENE 2

(MACBETH and LADY MACBETH enter)

MACBETH: Honey, I am really going wacky over all of this killing, greed, and guilt. What am I supposed to do?

LADY MACBETH: Be a man!

MACBETH: Right, what's done is done, there is no turning back now, and I will kill anyone that comes in my way! I must see those crazy witches!

(MACBETH and LADY MACBETH exit)

ACT 4 SCENE 1

(WITCHES enter with Cauldron)

WITCHES: Double, Double toil and trouble, Fire burn, and cauldron bubble.

WITCH #1: Eye of newt, and toe of frog, Wool of bat, and tongue of dog.

WITCH #2: Scale of dragon, tooth of wolf, Witches' mummy, maw and gulf.

WITCH #3: Adder's fork, and blind-worm's sting,
Lizard's leg, and howlet's wing.
By the pricking of my thumbs,
Something wicked this way comes.

(enter MACBETH)

MACBETH: How now, you secret, black, and midnight hags!
Tell me what I need to know!

WITCH #1: Macbeth, Macbeth, Macbeth, beware Macduff.

WITCH #2: None of woman born shall harm Macbeth.

WITCH #3: Macbeth will never die until the Great Birnam
Wood comes to High Dunsinane Hill

MACBETH: So let me get this straight: a forest that is miles
away from a hill has to actually move together, nobody born by
a woman can harm me, and I only have to beware of Macduff?

WITCHES: Yep. That's what we said, don't you listen?

MACBETH: *(to himself)* Cool. First I have to kill Macduff and
his family!

(ALL exit)

ACT 4 SCENE 2

(Enter MACDUFF and MALCOLM)

MACDUFF: Malcolm, we need to have you come back to Scotland so you can be king. I am not treacherous.

MALCOLM: Yeah, but Macbeth is. I hear Macbeth is being a
bully and a tyrant.

MACDUFF: I got the King of England to let me borrow his army
so we can go over and kick Macbeth's butt!

MALCOLM: Great!

(enter ROSS)

MALCOLM: Hello Ross.

MACDUFF: Hey, you just visited my family, how are they?

ROSS: Macbeth, well, he, ummm, has this murderer guy and.....

MACDUFF: No!

ROSS: Yes.

MACDUFF: AGGGHHHHHHHHHHHHHHH!!!!!!!!!!!

(MACDUFF runs of stage screaming and waving his sword)

MALCOLM: Wow, that's a bummer.

ROSS: Yeah.

(ROSS and MALCOLM exit)

ACT 5 SCENE 1

(enter LADY MACBETH sleep walking)

LADY MACBETH: *(in sleep walking voice)* Can't wash blood off hands. Out, damned spot! Out I say! Feel guilty about King Duncan, Banquo, Lady Macduff. Husband going nuts. *(repeats constantly untill she exits)*

ACT 5 SCENE 2

(enter MACBETH talking to himself)

MACBETH: I have to kill everyone, no one will stop me from being King. *(looks offstage as if he were looking out a window)* Well now that is weird. It appears that Birnam Woods is moving closer to our castle here on Dunsinane Hill.

(A loud scream from LADY MACBETH is heard off stage)

MACBETH: What was that? *(looks offstage)* Ahhh man, Lady Macbeth just died. Bummer. Out, out, brief candle! Life's but a walking shadow, a poor player that struts and frets his hour upon the stage and then is heard no more. Eh, she was bugging me anyway. Well, the witches have been right every time. But I think they are wrong this time. I will die fighting!

(enter Siward)

MACBETH: What do you want Young Siward?

SIWARD: I want to kill you Macbeth!

MACBETH: Funny you say that, I can't be killed by a man born from woman.

SIWARD: Uh oh.

(MACBETH kills Siward)

MACBETH: This is going to be easy.

(enter MACDUFF)

MACBETH: Well, well, well.

MACDUFF: That's a deep subject

MACBETH: I will have you know that I bear a charmed life. I cannot be killed by a man born from woman.

MACDUFF: Really, that's nice.

MACBETH: *(taken aback)* Why do you say that?

MACDUFF: Because I was plucked from my mom's womb. Achmmm.... what the witches REALLY meant was "no man NATURALLY born from a woman". Stinks to be you.

MACBETH: Uh oh.

(MACDUFF kills MACBETH)

MACDUFF: Hey Malcolm!

(MALCOLM and ROSS enter)

MALCOLM: Got him!

ROSS: *(talking to Malcolm)* Well you're King now!

MALCOLM: Great! And since you were all so brave, I pronounce you all Earls! *(MALCOLM and MACDUFF high five while everyone cheers)*

THE END

The 10-Minute or so Macbeth
By William Shakespeare
Creatively modified by Brendan P. Kelso
12-17+ Actors

CAST OF CHARACTERS

MACBETH – Thane of Glamis – the good guy, then the bad guy

LADY MACBETH – really evil wife of Macbeth

BANQUO – Macbeth's friend, then ex-friend

WITCHES* (#1, 2, & 3) – Scary witches with cool lines

ROSS – Thane of Ross

DUNCAN** – King of Scotland

MALCOLM – son of King Duncan

DONALBAIN – the other son of King Duncan

MACDUFF – Thane of Fife

LADY MACDUFF** – Macduff's wife

SON OF MACDUFF*** – Son of Macduff

CAPTAIN*** – a captain

MURDERER – a murderer and a really bad guy

SOLDIER** – a soldier

SIWARD** – an Earl

*1-3 witches can be played by 1-3 actors

** Duncan and Soldier can be played by the same actor

*** Lady Macduff and Siward can be played by the same actor

**** Captain and Son of Macduff can be played by the same actor

For more actors there can be extra: witches, murderers, soldiers, pets, trees, etc. – be creative!

ACT 1 SCENE 1

(WITCHES enter)

WITCHES: Fair is foul, and foul is fair;
Hover through the fog and filthy air.

WITCH #1: When shall we three meet again? In thunder, lightening, or in rain?

WITCH #2: When the hurlyburly's done, When the battle's lost and won.

WITCH #3: Wow, talk about confusion, what did we just say?

WITCH #1: Let's meet again after the war to talk with Macbeth.

WITCHES #3 & #2: Oh....Okay.

(WITCHES exit)

ACT 1 SCENE 2

(DUNCAN, MALCOLM, and DONALBAIN enter)

DUNCAN: Malcolm my son, I wonder what is going on with the war?

MALCOLM: I don't know, your highness, but look, there is a wounded young captain, maybe he knows.

(CAPTAIN enters)

CAPTAIN: *(bloody and delirious, kneels)* King of Scotland. There was lots of blood and bodies. The Thane of Cawdor is a traitor. But we were saved for brave Macbeth, well he deserves that name, killed them all and chased the Norwegians out of Scotland! ALL HAIL MACBETH! *(as he falls on his face and dies a miserable death)*

DONALBAIN: Awesome. *(DONALBAIN steps over body to talk to DUNCAN)* Hey Dad, here comes the worthy Thane of Ross.

(ROSS enters, steps over body)

DUNCAN: Great, Ross, go tell Macbeth that he is now the Thane of Cawdor.

ROSS: Will do.

DUNCAN: And get rid of this body!

ROSS: Yes, sir! *(ALL exit ROSS drags CAPTAIN'S body off stage)*

ACT 1 SCENE 3

(WITCHES enter and gather around the cauldron. WITCHES do various creepy and gross things)

(MACBETH and BANQUO enter a moment later)

BANQUO: You're my good buddy, Macbeth.

MACBETH: Mine too, Banquo.

BANQUO: Friends forever!

MACBETH: Yeah! *(they high five or do some other special handshake)*

BANQUO: Look at these crazy looking old hags. So withered and so wild in their attire.

MACBETH: Yeah, they're pretty creepy *(sniffs one)* and smelly too!

WITCHES: Hey Macbeth!

MACBETH: Yeah?

WITCH #1: All hail, Macbeth! hail to thee, Thane of Glamis!

WITCH #2: All hail, Macbeth! hail to thee, Thane of Cawdor!

WITCH #3: All hail, Macbeth! that shalt be King hereafter! Of Scotland that is!

BANQUO: That was cool! I want you to tell me my future too!

WITCH #2: Fine, ummm....all your sons will be kings!

BANQUO: Now that's a reading!

MACBETH: But I am only the Thane of Glamis?

WITCHES: Bye-Bye! *(WITCHES exit)*

BANQUO: Whoa! Where did they go? *(looking around)* Look, here comes the worthy Thane of Ross.

(ROSS enters)

MACBETH: Hey Ross.

ROSS: Hello, I have a message for you from the king.... *(reads from a very long sheet)* "You da man".

MACBETH: What does that mean?

ROSS: It means, since you saved our country, that you are now the Thane of Cawdor and you get all of his goods.

MACBETH: *(aside to audience)* Really....hmmm, those old ladies were right. I wonder what it would be like to be King, I wonder what I would have to do to be King.... oh this could be fun! Come what may.

BANQUO: Mac, what are you thinking over there?

MACBETH: Oh, nothing. *(said with a big fake smile)*

(ALL exit)

ACT 1 SCENE 4

(LADY MACBETH enters)

LADY MACBETH: *(reading letter)* "Dear honey, met some really weird old ladies, they said I would be King, bye." Hmmm-mmm....... *(thinking to herself evilly as she walks off stage)* must be mean, must be nasty, cruel, callous, evil, vicious, wicked, malicious, ...oh yeah, and did I mention mean!

(LADY MACBETH exits)

ACT 1 SCENE 5

(Enter DUNCAN, MALCOLM, DONALBAIN, MACBETH, and BANQUO)

DUNCAN: Well hello, Thane of Cawdor.

MACBETH: Hello!

DUNCAN: Just want to let you all know, that I am pronouncing my son Malcolm to be the next King when I step down.

MALCOLM: Yes!

MACBETH: *(aside)* No!

DUNCAN: What?

MACBETH: Nothing.

DONALBAIN: Good job, brother.

MACBETH: *(aside to audience)* Now I have to go through the king and his son. Man, this is going to get messy. Remember, look like the innocent flower, but be the serpent under't.

BANQUO: Mac, what are you thinking over there?

MACBETH: Oh, nothing. *(said with a big fake smile)*

(ALL exit)

ACT 1 SCENE 6

(MACBETH enters; LADY MACBETH is center)

MACBETH: Hi Honey, I'm home!

LADY MACBETH: Okay, I have a plan for you to be king! *(as she snickers evilly)*

MACBETH: Okay.

LADY MACBETH: King's coming over tonight for dinner, I will be serving him a large helping of "your goose is cooked", if you know what I mean.

MACBETH: *(confused)* Ahhh. No, I don't know what you mean.

LADY MACBETH: I am going to serve him his "last meal". If you know what I mean.

MACBETH: Right! *(confused)* Wrong, I don't know what you mean.

LADY MACBETH: *(frustrated)* I am going to serve him food and you are going to kill him. Do you NOW know what I mean?

MACBETH: Right!

(LADY MACBETH and MACBETH laugh together evilly and make evil faces towards the audience. There is a loud knocking.)

LADY MACBETH: That's the king, put on a happy face and let's go!

(both exit)

ACT 1 SCENE 7

(MACBETH, LADY MACBETH, DUNCAN, MALCOLM, DONALBAIN, BANQUO are all sitting around eating dinner)

DUNCAN: Great meal, Lady Macbeth, you have to send me that recipe.

BANQUO: That really was a great meal.

DONALBAIN: It sure was!

LADY MACBETH: Well, I am glad you enjoyed it. Oh my, look at the time, everyone go to sleep! *(LADY MACBETH shoos everyone out of the room)*

ALL: Okay.

ACT 1 SCENE 8

MACBETH: *(to himself alone on stage)* To be or not to be...... whoops, wrong play. To kill or not to kill.....there we go....if I kill him lots of people will hate me, BUT, if I kill him I will be King. Hmmmm – to kill or not to kill....... *(LADY MACBETH enters)*

LADY MACBETH: So, did you do it?

MACBETH: *(taking a stand)* I have decided that I am not going to do it.

LADY MACBETH: WHAT!? Are you a man? Get on with it!

MACBETH: *(whining)* But do I have to?

LADY MACBETH: Listen here, pull yourself together and go do the deed. I will get the bodyguards drunk and then we will blame them.

MACBETH: Yes, dear. *(as LADY MACBETH puts his dagger in his hands and shoves him off stage)*

ACT 2 SCENE 1

(DUNCAN runs on stage and dies with a dagger stuck in him, MACBETH drags his body off and then returns with the bloody dagger. LADY MACBETH enters)

LADY MACBETH: Did you do it?

MACBETH: *(clueless)* Do what?

LADY MACBETH: KILL HIM!

MACBETH: Oh yeah, all done. I have done the deed.

LADY MACBETH: *(pointing at the dagger)* What is that?

MCABETH: What?

LADY MACBETH: Why do you still have the bloody dagger with you?

MACBETH: Ummmmm, I don't know.

LADY MACBETH: Well go put it back!

MACBETH: NO! I'm scared of the dark, and there is a dead body in there.

LADY MACBETH: Man you are a wimp, give it to me. *(LADY MACBETH takes the dagger, exits, and returns)*

LADY MACBETH: All done.

(there is a loud knock at the door)

LADY MACBETH: It's 2am! This really is not a good time for more visitors. *(goes to the door)* Who is it? *(opens door)*

MACDUFF: It is Macduff, I am here to see the king.

MACBETH: He is sleeping in there.

(MACDUFF exits)

MACDUFF: *(off stage scream)* AGHHHHHHHHHHH – He's dead, he's dead!!! *(MACDUFF enters)*

MACBETH: Who?

MACDUFF: Who do you think? *(they both scream)*

BANQUO: *(BANQUO, MALCOLM, and DONALBAIN enter)* What happened?

MACDUFF: The king has been murdered.

MALCOLM & DONALBAIN: Aghhhhhhhh!!!!!!!!

DONALBAIN: We must be next.

MALCOLM: Let's get out of here.

DONALBAIN: I'm heading to Ireland.

MALCOLM: I'm off to England. *(MALCOLM and DONALBAIN exit)*

PlayingWithPlays.com

MACDUFF: Well, since there is no one left to be King, why don't you do it Mac?

LADY MACBETH & MACBETH: Okay. *(LADY MACBETH, MACBETH and MACDUFF exit)*

BANQUO: *(To himself)* I fear, Thou play'dst most foully for't. *(MACBETH returns)*

MACBETH: Bank, what are you thinking over there?

BANQUO: Oh, nothing. *(said with a big fake smile)* Gotta go! See ya! *(BANQUO exits)*

MACBETH: I don't trust Banquo, he knows too much. *(towards offstage)* Hey, Murderer!

MURDERER: *(MURDERER enters)* Yes, sir?

MACBETH: Banquo *(makes slash across throat sign)*

MURDERER: Gotcha *(MURDERER and MACBETH exit)*

ACT 3 SCENE 1

(BANQUO is standing on stage tying his shoe or something like that. MURDERER enters)

MURDERER: Hey, you Banquo?

BANQUO: Yeah, who are you?

MURDERER: Murderer.

BANQUO: Uh oh.

(BANQUO is killed)

ACT 3 SCENE 2

(MACBETH and LADY MACBETH enter)

MACBETH: Honey, I am really going wacky over all of this killing, greed, and guilt. What am I supposed to do?

LADY MACBETH: Be a man!

MACBETH: Right, what's done is done, there is no turning back now, and I will kill anyone that comes in my way! I must see those crazy witches!

(MACBETH and LADY MACBETH exit)

ACT 4 SCENE 1

(WITCHES enter with Cauldron)

WITCHES: Double, Double toil and trouble,
Fire burn, and cauldron bubble.

WITCH #1: Eye of newt, and toe of frog,
Wool of bat, and tongue of dog.

WITCH #2: Scale of dragon, tooth of wolf,
Witches' mummy, maw and gulf.

WITCH #3: Adder's fork, and blind-worm's sting,
Lizard's leg, and howlet's wing.
By the pricking of my thumbs,
Something wicked this way comes.

(enter MACBETH)

MACBETH: How now, you secret, black, and midnight hags!
Tell me what I need to know!

WITCH #1: Macbeth, Macbeth, Macbeth, beware Macduff.

WITCH #2: None of woman born shall harm Macbeth.

WITCH #3: Macbeth will never die until the Great Birnam Wood comes to High Dunsinane Hill

MACBETH: So let me get this straight: a forest that is miles away from a hill has to actually move together, nobody born by a woman can harm me, and I only have to beware of Macduff?

WITCHES: Yep. That's what we said, don't you listen?

MACBETH: *(to himself)* Cool. First I have to kill Macduff and his family!

(ALL exit)

ACT 4 SCENE 2

(Enter ROSS, LADY MACDUFF, and SON OF MACDUFF)

LADY MACDUFF: Ross, I am mad at my husband because he left his family behind like this.

ROSS: Lady Macduff, I just want you to know that your husband, Macduff, has headed to England to try and save Scotland.

SON OF MACDUFF: Mom, I thought you said dad was a traitor and left us?

LADY MACDUFF: I guess I was wrong!

ROSS: *(yelling to offstage)* Oh, by the way, I hear trouble is brewing, you should leave soon, and I mean VERY soon. Bye! *(ROSS exits)*

LADY MACDUFF: Why should I fly? I have done no harm. Don't worry, we will leave soon.

(enter MURDERER)

MURDERER: Hello.

LADY MACDUFF: Who are you?

MURDERER: Murderer.

SON and LADY MACDUFF: Uh oh. *(LADY MACDUFF and SON run offstage in opposite directions. MURDERER chases LADY MACDUFF. Suddenly a loud scream is heard. LADY MACDUFF stumbles on stage with a dagger in her, dies.)*

(ROSS enters)

ROSS: Ouch, that looked like it hurt, I tried to warn you. I think I will go tell Macduff about this, boy is he going to be bummed. *(ROSS exits dragging LADY MACDUFF off stage)*

ACT 4 SCENE 3

(Enter MACDUFF and MALCOLM)

MACDUFF: Malcolm, we need to have you come back to Scotland so you can be king. I am not treacherous.

MALCOLM: Yeah, but Macbeth is. I hear Macbeth is being a bully and a tyrant.

MACDUFF: I got the King of England to let me borrow his army so we can go over and kick Macbeth's butt.

MALCOLM: Great!

(enter ROSS)

MALCOLM: Hello Ross.

MACDUFF: Hey, how's my family?

ROSS: Macbeth.

MACDUFF: No!

ROSS: Yes.

MACDUFF: AGGGHHHHHHHHHHHHHHHH!!!!!!!!!!!!

(MACDUFF runs of stage screaming and waving his sword)

MALCOLM: Wow, that's a bummer.

ROSS: Yeah.

(ROSS and MALCOLM exit)

ACT 5 SCENE 1

(enter LADY MACBETH sleep walking)

LADY MACBETH: *(in sleep walking voice)* Can't wash blood off hands. Out, damned spot! Out I say! Feel guilty about King Duncan, Banquo, Lady Macduff. Husband going nuts. *(repeats constantly untill she exits)*

ACT 5 SCENE 2

(enter MACBETH talking to himself)

MACBETH: I have to kill everyone, no one will stop me from being King.

(enter SOLDIER – scared)

SOLDIER: Umm, sir?

MACBETH: What do you want, soldier?

SOLDIER: Well, the weirdest thing has happened. It appears that Birnam Woods is moving closer to our castle here on Dunsinane Hill. Oh yeah, and all of your army guys are scared of you and are deserting their posts.

(A loud scream from LADY MACBETH is heard off stage)

MACBETH: What was that?

SOLDIER: Oh, Lady Macbeth just died.

MACBETH: Bummer. *(To himself)* Out, out, brief candle! Life's but a walking shadow, a poor player that struts and frets his hour upon the stage and then is heard no more. Eh, she was bugging me anyway.

SOLDIER: huh?

MACBETH: Guess you can't win them all. Oh by the way, soldier.

SOLDIER: Yes? *(MACBETH kills soldier)* Ouch! Why did you do that?

MACBETH: I didn't like all the news you told me.

SOLDIER: Oh. *(falls over dead)*

MACBETH: *(to himself)* Well, the witches have been right every time. But I think they are wrong this time. I will die fighting!

(enter Siward)

MACBETH: What do you want Young Siward?

SIWARD: I want to kill you, Macbeth!

MACBETH: Funny you say that, I can't be killed by a man born from woman.

SIWARD: Uh oh.

(MACBETH kills Siward)

MACBETH: This is going to be easy.

(enter MACDUFF)

MACBETH: Well, well, well.

MACDUFF: That's a deep subject.

MACBETH: I will have you know that I bear a charmed life. I cannot be killed by a man born from woman.

MACDUFF: Really, that's nice.

MACBETH: *(taken aback)* Why do you say that?

MACDUFF: Because I was plucked from my mom's womb. Achmmm.... what the witches REALLY meant was "no man NATURALLY born from a woman". Stinks to be you.

MACBETH: Uh oh.

(MACDUFF kills MACBETH)

MACDUFF: Hey Malcolm!

(MALCOLM, DONALBAIN, and ROSS enter)

DONALBAIN: Got him!

ROSS: *(talking to Malcolm)* Well, you're King now!

MALCOLM: Great! And since you were all so brave, I pronounce you all Earls! *(MALCOLM and DONALBAIN high five while everyone cheers)*

THE END

12275920R00024

Printed in Great Britain
by Amazon.co.uk, Ltd.,
Marston Gate.